Learn Hindi for Beginners

Basic Hindi Simplified for You

Written By: Khushi S.

Published By: My First Picture Book Inc.

Copyright: My First Picture Book Inc. © 2023 · All Rights Reserved

Table of Contents

Chapter 1: Introduction to Hindi Language 1
Chapter 2: Alphabet and Pronunciation 3
Chapter 3: Greetings and Basic Conversation 8
    Greetings 8
    Introductions 9
    Basic Conversation 10
    Farewells 12
Chapter 4: Numbers and Counting 13
    Numbers 13
    Counting 15
Chapter 5: Grammar Basics 17
Chapter 6: Adjectives and Adverbs 21
    Adjectives 21
    Adverbs 24
Chapter 7: Verbs and Tenses 27
    Verbs 27
    Tenses 30
Chapter 8: Nouns and Articles 33
    Nouns 33
    Articles 36
Chapter 9: Questions and Negation 38
    Questions 38
    Negation 41
Chapter 10: Idioms and Expressions 44

Idioms 44

Expressions 46

Chapter 11: Writing System 48

Chapter 12: Honorfics in Hindi 51

Chapter 13: Slang and Colloquialisms 53

Chapter 14: Hindi Vocabulary 55

Animals vocabulary 55

Family vocabulary 56

Time vocabulary 57

Colors vocabulary 58

Shapes vocabulary 59

Weather vocabulary 60

Transportation vocabulary 61

Food vocabulary 62

Fruits vocabulary 63

Vegetables vocabulary 64

Emotions vocabulary 65

Chapter 1: Introduction to Hindi Language

Hindi is an Indo-Aryan language spoken mainly in India, as well as in some other countries such as Nepal, Fiji, Mauritius, and Trinidad and Tobago. It is one of the official languages of India, alongside English, and is the fourth most spoken language in the world, with over 600 million speakers.

Hindi uses the Devanagari script, which consists of 47 primary characters and is written from left to right. The language has a rich literary tradition, with works spanning from ancient Indian texts such as the Vedas and the Mahabharata to modern-day literature and cinema.

Hindi is closely related to other Indo-Aryan languages, such as Punjabi, Gujarati, and Bengali, and also shares many similarities with Urdu, another Indo-Aryan language spoken in Pakistan and India.

History and Origins: Hindi is believed to have evolved from a proto-language known as Sanskrit. It emerged as a distinct language around the 7th century CE and was influenced by various languages such as Persian, Arabic, and Turkish. Modern Standard Hindi is based on the Khari Boli dialect spoken in Delhi and surrounding areas.

Regional Variations: Hindi has several dialects and regional variations, each with its own unique vocabulary, pronunciation, and grammar. Some of the major dialects include Braj Bhasha, Awadhi, and Bhojpuri, while Hindi spoken in different regions of India such as Mumbai, Kolkata, and Chennai may have distinct features as well.

Vocabulary: Hindi vocabulary is largely derived from Sanskrit and Prakrit, as well as from Persian, Arabic, and English. The language has a rich repertoire of nouns, verbs, adjectives, adverbs, and other parts of speech.

Writing System: Hindi is written in the Devanagari script, which is also used for several other languages such as Marathi, Nepali, and Sanskrit. The script consists of 47 characters, each representing a syllable, and is written from left to right.

Grammar: Hindi grammar is complex and has several features that may be challenging for learners, such as gender distinctions, cases for nouns, and complex verb conjugation. However, with practice and guidance, it is possible to develop a good command of the language.

Chapter 2: Alphabet and Pronunciation

The Hindi alphabet is based on the Devanagari script, which consists of 47 primary characters, including 14 vowels and 33 consonants. The script is written from left to right, and each character represents a syllable. Here's an overview of the Hindi alphabet:

Vowels: There are 14 vowels in Hindi, including both short and long sounds. The short vowels are अ (a), इ (i), उ (u), ए (e), and ओ (o), while the long vowels are आ (aa), ई (ii), ऊ (uu), ऐ (ai), and औ (au). Additionally, there are three diphthongs in Hindi, which are combinations of two vowels: अय (ay), अव (av), and उय (uy).

Here's an overview of the Hindi vowels:

अ (a) - This is the most basic and neutral vowel in Hindi, and is pronounced with the mouth open and the tongue low in the mouth.

आ (aa) - This is the long sound of अ (a), and is pronounced with the mouth more open and the tongue slightly lower than for अ (a). It is held for a longer duration than the short अ (a).

इ (i) - This vowel is pronounced with the tongue touching the roof of the mouth just behind the front teeth. It is a short vowel, and is pronounced with the mouth slightly more closed than for अ (a).

ई (ii) - This is the long sound of इ (i), and is pronounced with the mouth more closed and the tongue higher in the mouth than for इ (i). It is held for a longer duration than the short इ (i).

उ (u) - This vowel is pronounced with the lips rounded and the tongue positioned at the back of the mouth. It is a short vowel, and is pronounced with the mouth slightly more open than for इ (i).

ऊ (uu) - This is the long sound of उ (u), and is pronounced with the lips more rounded and the tongue positioned further back in the mouth than for उ (u). It is held for a longer duration than the short उ (u).

ऋ (r̥) - This vowel is pronounced with the tongue curled backwards and touching the roof of the mouth. It is a short vowel, and is used mostly in Sanskrit loanwords.

ॠ (r̥̄) - This is the long sound of ऋ (r̥), and is pronounced with the tongue curled backwards and touching the roof of the mouth for a longer duration than the short ऋ (r̥).

ए (e) - This vowel is pronounced with the tongue positioned midway between the front and back of the mouth. It is a short vowel, and is pronounced with the mouth slightly more open than for इ (i).

ऐ (ai) - This is the long sound of ए (e), and is pronounced with the mouth more open and the tongue positioned higher in the mouth than for ए (e). It is held for a longer duration than the short ए (e).

ओ (o) - This vowel is pronounced with the tongue positioned midway between the front and back of the mouth, and with the lips rounded. It is a short vowel, and is pronounced with the mouth slightly more open than for उ (u).

औ (au) - This is the long sound of ओ (o), and is pronounced with the mouth more open and the lips more rounded than for ओ (o). It is held for a longer duration than the short ओ (o).

अय (ay) - This is a diphthong in Hindi, and is pronounced by combining the short अ (a) sound with the short इ (i) sound.

अव (av) - This is another diphthong in Hindi, and is pronounced by combining the short अ (a) sound with the short उ (u) sound.

Consonants: There are 33 consonants in Hindi, which are divided into five groups based on their pronunciation: velar, palatal, retroflex, dental, and labial. Some examples of each group include:

1. Velar Consonants:
- क (ka)
- ख (kha)
- ग (ga)
- घ (gha)
- ङ (nga)

2. Palatal Consonants:
- च (cha)
- छ (chha)
- ज (ja)
- झ (jha)
- ञ (nya)

3. Retroflex Consonants:
- ट (Ta)
- ठ (Tha)
- ड (Da)
- ढ (Dha)
- ण (na)

4. Dental Consonants:
   - त (ta)
   - थ (tha)
   - द (da)
   - ध (dha)
   - न (na)

5. Labial Consonants:
   - प (pa)
   - फ (pha)
   - ब (ba)
   - भ (bha)
   - म (ma)

6. Semi-Vowels:
   - य (ya)
   - र (ra)
   - ल (la)
   - व (va)

7. Glottal Consonants:
   - अंग्रेज़ी उच्चारण के लिए "h" (ha)

Diacritical Marks: Hindi also uses diacritical marks, or matras, to modify the pronunciation of certain vowels and consonants. For example, the matra ि (i) placed above a consonant changes its pronunciation to the corresponding palatal sound, while the matra ु (u) placed below a consonant changes its pronunciation to the corresponding retroflex sound.

Pronunciation: Hindi pronunciation can be challenging for learners, as it involves several distinct sounds that may not exist in their native language. Some of the key pronunciation features to keep in mind include:

- Vowels are pronounced distinctly and should be given their full value, whether short or long.
- Consonants are pronounced with aspiration, meaning that there is a small puff of air released when they are pronounced. This can be heard as a slight puff of air when pronouncing consonants like क (ka) and त (ta).
- Some consonants are pronounced with a retroflex sound, which involves curling the tongue slightly backwards. This is particularly true of the retroflex consonants, as well as the letters ट (Ta) and ड (Da).
- Some consonants are pronounced with an emphasis on the aspiration, giving them a breathy or whispered quality. This is particularly true of the letters फ (pha), ख (kha), ठ (Tha), and छ (chha).

Vowel Harmony: Hindi follows a system of vowel harmony, which means that certain vowels can only be combined with other specific vowels. For example, the vowel इ (i) can only be combined with the vowels ए (e) and ओ (o), while the vowel उ (u) can only be combined with the vowels ऐ (ai) and औ (au). This system can help to make pronunciation easier and more consistent.

Nasalization: Hindi also uses nasalization, which involves pronouncing certain sounds with the air flowing through the nose. Nasalization is indicated in writing by adding the nasalization symbol ঁ (chandrabindu) above a vowel. Examples of nasalized sounds in Hindi include the sounds in the words अंगूर (grape) and दंत (tooth).

Stress: Unlike some other languages, Hindi does not have a system of stress or emphasis on certain syllables within a word. Instead, each syllable is pronounced with roughly equal emphasis.

Chapter 3: Greetings and Basic Conversation

Greetings

In Hindi, it is common to greet people with respect by adding "ji" to the end of their name. For example, if someone's name is "Raj," you could greet them as "Raj ji" to show respect.

Another way to greet someone in Hindi is by using the phrase "kaise ho?" which means "how are you?" This is a more casual greeting and is often used among friends and family.

In Hindi, it is common to use the phrase "kya haal hai?" to ask "how are you?" in a casual setting. This phrase can be used to greet friends, family members, and peers.

When greeting someone in Hindi, it is important to use the correct honorifics to show respect. For example, if you are greeting an older person, you would use "aap" instead of "tum" to address them.

नमस्ते (namaste) - This is a common greeting in Hindi that is used in formal settings. It can be translated as "Hello" or "Greetings" and is often accompanied by a slight bow with the hands pressed together in front of the chest.

नमस्कार (namaskaar) - Similar to नमस्ते (namaste), नमस्कार (namaskaar) is a formal greeting that can be used to say "Hello" or "Greetings" in Hindi.

हाय (haay) - This is a more informal greeting in Hindi that is similar to "Hi" in English. It is often used among friends, family, or peers.

Introductions

When introducing yourself in Hindi, it is polite to say "main" before your name, which means "I am." For example, you could say "Main Anjali hoon," which means "I am Anjali."

In Hindi, there are different words for "you" depending on the level of formality. "Aap" is a formal word for "you" and is used when addressing elders, superiors, or strangers. "Tum" is an informal word for "you" and is used when addressing friends or family members who are younger or of the same age.

In Hindi, it is common to ask someone where they are from as a way of starting a conversation. For example, you could ask "aap kahan se ho?" which means "where are you from?"

When introducing yourself in Hindi, it is polite to add "ji" to the end of your name as a way of showing respect. For example, you could say "mera naam Anjali ji hai" to introduce yourself.

मेरा नाम है (mera naam hai) - This phrase is used to introduce oneself in Hindi, and can be translated as "My name is."

आपका नाम क्या है? (aapka naam kya hai?) - This is a formal way to ask someone's name in Hindi, and can be translated as "What is your name?"

तुम्हारा नाम क्या है? (tumhara naam kya hai?) - This is an informal way to ask someone's name in Hindi, and can be translated as "What is your name?"

Basic Conversation

In Hindi, it is common to ask people about their family members as a way of showing interest and building rapport. For example, you could ask "aapke parivar mein kaun-kaun hain?" which means "who all are there in your family?"

Hindi is a gendered language, so it is important to use the correct gender when addressing people. For example, if you are talking to a man, you would use masculine words like "woh" to refer to him, and if you are talking to a woman, you would use feminine words like "woh" to refer to her.

When responding to questions in Hindi, it is common to use the affirmative word "haan" to mean "yes," and the negative word "nahi" to mean "no."

In Hindi, it is common to ask people about their work or occupation as a way of showing interest and getting to know them. For example, you could ask "aap kya kaam karte hain?" which means "what is your profession?"

When speaking in Hindi, it is important to use the correct gender agreement when referring to people and things. For example, if you are referring to a male teacher, you would use the word "adhyapak," which is a masculine noun.

क्या हाल है? (kya haal hai?) - This is a common way to ask "How are you?" in Hindi. It is often used in informal settings among friends and family.

आप कैसे हैं? (aap kaise hain?) - This is a formal way to ask "How are you?" in Hindi. It is often used in professional or formal settings.

ठीक हूँ, धन्यवाद। (theek hoon, dhanyavaad) - This phrase can be used to say "I am fine, thank you" in Hindi.

आपसे मिलकर खुशी हुई। (aapse milkar khushi hui) - This is a formal way to say "Nice to meet you" in Hindi.

तुमसे मिलकर खुशी हुई। (tumse milkar khushi hui) - This is an informal way to say "Nice to meet you" in Hindi.

मुझे यह समझ नहीं आ रहा है। (mujhe yah samajh nahi aa raha hai) - This phrase can be used to say "I don't understand" in Hindi.

क्या आपको हिंदी बोलना आता है? (kya aapko Hindi bolna aata hai?) - This is a formal way to ask "Do you speak Hindi?" in Hindi.

तुम हिंदी बोलते हो? (tum Hindi bolte ho?) - This is an informal way to ask "Do you speak Hindi?" in Hindi.

Farewells

In Hindi, it is common to use the word "namaste" as a farewell, especially in more formal settings. This is a way of showing respect and acknowledging the other person's presence.

Another way to say "goodbye" in Hindi is by using the phrase "fir milenge," which means "see you later." This is a more casual way of saying goodbye and is often used among friends and family.

In Hindi, it is common to use the phrase "shubh raatri" to say "good night" as a farewell. This phrase can be used in both formal and informal settings.

When saying goodbye in Hindi, it is common to add "phir milenge" to indicate that you will meet the person again. This phrase can be used to express a sense of hope and connection.

अलविदा (alvida) - This is a common way to say "Goodbye" in Hindi.

फिर मिलेंगे (phir milenge) - This phrase can be used to say "See you later" in Hindi.

शुभ रात्रि (shubh ratri) - This phrase can be used to say "Goodnight" in Hindi.

शुभ प्रभात (shubh prabhaat) - This phrase can be used to say "Good morning" in Hindi.

शुभ संध्या (shubh sandhya) - This phrase can be used to say "Good evening" in Hindi.

Chapter 4: Numbers and Counting

Numbers

Hindi numbers are based on the decimal system, which means that the numbers are organized in groups of ten. The Hindi numerals are written in the Devanagari script and consist of ten digits. Here are the Hindi numerals from 1 to 20:

1 - एक (ek)
2 - दो (do)
3 - तीन (teen)
4 - चार (chaar)
5 - पाँच (paanch)
6 - छह (chhah)
7 - सात (saat)
8 - आठ (aath)
9 - नौ (nau)
10 - दस (das)
11 - ग्यारह (gyaarah)
12 - बारह (baarh)
13 - तेरह (terah)
14 - चौदह (chaudah)
15 - पंद्रह (pandrah)
16 - सोलह (solah)
17 - सत्रह (satrah)
18 - अठारह (atharah)
19 - उन्नीस (unnis)
20 - बीस (bees)

To form numbers from 21 to 99, the Hindi numerals for 20, 30, 40, etc. are combined with the unit digit, as follows:

21 - इक्कीस (ikkees)
22 - बाईस (baais)
23 - तेईस (teis)
24 - चौबीस (chaubees)
25 - पच्चीस (pachhees)
26 - छब्बीस (chhabbees)
27 - सताईस (sattaais)
28 - अट्ठाईस (attahais)
29 - उनतीस (untis)
30 - तीस (tees)
40 - चालीस (chaalis)
50 - पचास (pachaas)
60 - साठ (saath)
70 - सत्तर (sattar)
80 - अस्सी (assi)
90 - नब्बे (nabbe)
99 - नवासी (navaasi)

To form numbers above 100, the Hindi word for hundred (सौ - sau) is used, followed by the number. For example, 101 is "एक सौ एक" (ek sau ek), and 200 is "दो सौ" (do sau).

In Hindi, numbers can be formed up to trillions (10^{12}). To form numbers beyond thousands, the Hindi word for thousand (हजार - hazaar) is used, followed by the number. For example, 1,000 is "एक हजार" (ek hazaar), and 10,000 is "दस हजार" (das hazaar).

To form numbers beyond millions, the Hindi word for million (करोड़ - crore) is used, followed by the number. For example, 1,000,000 is "एक करोड़" (ek crore), and 10,000,000 is "दस करोड़" (das crore).

Counting

In Hindi, to count objects, the Hindi word for the number is used, followed by the noun. For example, to say "two books" in Hindi, you would say "दो किताबें" (do kitaaben).

In Hindi, the noun is usually pluralized by adding "एं" (en) to the end of the noun. For example, the singular noun for "book" is "किताब" (kitaab), and the plural noun is "किताबें" (kitaaben).

Here are some of the key terms you may come across when dealing with large numbers in Hindi:

- लाख (lakh): One lakh in Hindi represents 100,000. For example, if you want to say "one lakh rupees" in Hindi, you would say "एक लाख रुपये" (ek lakh rupaye).

- करोड़ (crore): One crore in Hindi represents 10,000,000. For example, if you want to say "ten crore rupees" in Hindi, you would say "दस करोड़ रुपये" (das crore rupaye).

- अरब (arab): One arab in Hindi represents 1,000,000,000.

To understand the difference between these large numbers and other numbers in Hindi, it is important to know that the word for "thousand" in Hindi is "हजार" (hazaar). So, for example, 1,000 in Hindi is "एक हजार" (ek hazaar), and 10,000 in Hindi is "दस हजार" (das hazaar).

To form larger numbers beyond thousands, the Hindi word for thousand (हजार - hazaar) is used, followed by the number. For example, 100,000 is "एक लाख" (ek lakh), and 1,000,000 is "दस लाख" (das lakh).

To form numbers beyond millions, the Hindi word for million (करोड़ - crore) is used, followed by the number. For example, 10,000,000 is "दस करोड़" (das crore), and 100,000,000 is "एक अरब" (ek arab).

Chapter 5: Grammar Basics

Parts of Speech: Hindi language has eight parts of speech, which include nouns, pronouns, verbs, adjectives, adverbs, prepositions, conjunctions, and interjections.

Gender: Hindi language has two genders, masculine and feminine. The gender of a noun is important as it affects the form of adjectives and verbs used to describe it.

Number: Hindi language has two numbers, singular and plural. The plural form is formed by adding -एं (-en) or -ओं (-on) to the singular form.

Case: Hindi language has three cases, subjective, objective, and possessive. The case of a noun or pronoun determines its function in a sentence.

Verbs: Hindi verbs are inflected for tense, aspect, mood, person, and number. Hindi language has three tenses, present, past, and future.

Sentence Structure: Hindi sentences follow a subject-object-verb (SOV) word order. The subject is usually placed at the beginning of the sentence, followed by the object, and then the verb.

Adjectives: Hindi adjectives must agree in gender, number, and case with the noun they modify. They usually follow the noun they modify.

Postpositions: Hindi language uses postpositions instead of prepositions to show the relationship between nouns in a sentence.

Pronouns: Hindi pronouns are inflected for gender, number, and case. There are several different types of pronouns in Hindi, including personal, possessive, demonstrative, and interrogative.

Conjuncts: Hindi language uses conjuncts, which are combinations of two or more consonants, to represent sounds that are not present in the Devanagari script. Conjuncts are an important part of Hindi writing and are often used in the middle or at the end of words.

Nouns: Hindi nouns are inflected for gender, number, and case. The gender of a noun determines the form of the adjective that modifies it. There are two numbers in Hindi, singular and plural. Nouns in Hindi can be classified into five different categories based on their gender and ending.

Case: Hindi has three cases, which are subjective, objective, and possessive. The subjective case is used for the subject of a sentence, the objective case is used for the object of a sentence, and the possessive case is used to indicate possession or ownership.

Verbs: Hindi verbs are inflected for tense, aspect, mood, person, and number. There are three tenses in Hindi, which are present, past, and future. The aspect of a verb can be perfective or imperfective, and the mood can be indicative, subjunctive, or imperative.

Adjectives: Hindi adjectives agree with the noun they modify in gender, number, and case. Adjectives in Hindi are usually placed after the noun they modify. Adjectives in Hindi can also function as nouns when they are used with the suffix "-वाला" (-wala).

Pronouns: Hindi pronouns are inflected for gender, number, and case. Personal pronouns in Hindi include the first, second, and third person. Hindi also has possessive, demonstrative, and interrogative pronouns.

Prepositions: Hindi uses postpositions instead of prepositions. Postpositions are added to the end of a noun or pronoun to show its relationship to another word in the sentence.

Conjunctions: Hindi has two types of conjunctions, coordinating and subordinating. Coordinating conjunctions join two or more words, phrases, or clauses of equal rank, while subordinating conjunctions join a dependent clause to an independent clause.

Interjections: Hindi interjections are used to express emotions, feelings, or attitudes. Interjections are not inflected for gender, number, or case.

Word Order: In Hindi, the typical word order for a simple sentence is subject-object-verb (SOV). This means that the subject comes first, followed by the object, and then the verb. However, this order can be changed for emphasis or to indicate a question.

Verb Agreement: Hindi verbs must agree in tense, aspect, mood, person, and number with the subject of the sentence. This means that the verb form changes based on who or what is performing the action.

Inflection: In Hindi, words change their form to indicate different grammatical functions. For example, nouns change form to indicate gender, number, and case, and verbs change form to indicate tense, aspect, mood, person, and number.

Compound Words: Hindi has many compound words, which are created by combining two or more words to form a new word. These compound words can be made up of nouns, adjectives, or verbs.

Reduplication: In Hindi, words can be repeated or partially repeated to indicate intensity, emphasis, or a change in meaning. For example, the word "mukti" (liberation) can be reduplicated to "mukt-mukt" to indicate complete liberation.

Honorifics: Hindi has a complex system of honorifics, which are used to show respect or politeness to different people. These honorifics can be added to nouns, pronouns, and verbs to indicate the level of respect or politeness required.

Sandhi: In Hindi, words can change form when they are combined with other words in a sentence. This process is known as sandhi, and it involves changes to the beginning, end, or middle of words to make them easier to pronounce.

Chapter 6: Adjectives and Adverbs

Adjectives

Adjectives are an important part of speech in Hindi, used to modify and describe nouns in a sentence. Here are some details about Hindi adjectives:

Agreement: In Hindi, adjectives must agree with the noun they modify in gender, number, and case. For example, if the noun is masculine and singular, the adjective modifying it must also be masculine and singular.

Position: In Hindi, adjectives usually follow the noun they modify. However, they can also be placed before the noun for emphasis or to create a specific effect in a sentence.

Types: Hindi adjectives can be classified into two main categories: descriptive and demonstrative. Descriptive adjectives describe the quality or attribute of a noun, while demonstrative adjectives indicate which noun is being referred to.

Comparison: Hindi adjectives can be used to compare two or more things. The comparative form of an adjective is formed by adding -तर (tar) to the end of the adjective. The superlative form is formed by adding -तम (tam) to the end of the adjective.

Forms: In Hindi, some adjectives change form to indicate tense or mood. For example, the adjective अच्छा (accha, good) changes to अच्छे (acche) in the plural form, and to अच्छी (acchi) in the feminine form.

Possessives: Hindi adjectives can also be used to indicate possession or ownership. For example, उसकी किताब (uski kitaab) means "her book".

Usage: Hindi adjectives can be used to describe the physical characteristics of a noun, such as its size, shape, color, and texture. They can also be used to describe a noun's emotional or psychological attributes, such as its mood, attitude, or personality.

Gender: In Hindi, adjectives must agree with the gender of the noun they modify. Masculine adjectives end in ा (aa) or उ (u), while feminine adjectives end in ी (ee) or इ (i). For example, सुंदर (sundar, beautiful) is a masculine adjective, while सुंदरी (sundari, beautiful) is a feminine adjective.

Number: In Hindi, adjectives must also agree with the number of the noun they modify. Singular adjectives end in ा (aa) or ाव (aav), while plural adjectives end in े (e) or ाएं (aayein). For example, लंबा (lamba, tall) is a singular adjective, while लंबे (lambe, tall) is a plural adjective.

Case: In Hindi, adjectives must also agree with the case of the noun they modify. For example, in the subjective case, the adjective must agree with the gender, number, and case of the subject of the sentence.

Emphasis: In Hindi, adjectives can be placed before the noun they modify to create emphasis or to create a specific effect in a sentence. For example, the sentence बच्चा खुश (bachcha khush, the child is happy) can be changed to खुश बच्चा (khush bachcha, the happy child) to emphasize the child's happiness.

Inflection: In Hindi, some adjectives can be inflected to indicate different degrees of intensity or comparison. For example, the adjective सुंदर (sundar, beautiful) can be inflected to सुंदरता (sundarta, beauty) to indicate the abstract quality of beauty.

Compound Adjectives: Hindi also has compound adjectives, which are formed by combining two or more adjectives to form a new word. For example, the compound adjective गोल-मटोल (gol-matol, round and chubby) combines the adjectives गोल (gol, round) and मटोल (matol, chubby) to describe a person or object.

Here are some examples of adjectives in Hindi:

- सुंदर (Sundar) - beautiful
- बड़ा (Bada) - big
- छोटा (Chhota) - small
- लंबा (Lamba) - long
- नारंगी (Naarangi) - orange
- नीला (Neela) - blue
- लाल (Laal) - red
- पीला (Peela) - yellow
- सफेद (Safed) - white
- काला (Kaala) - black
- गरम (Garam) - hot
- ठंडा (Thanda) - cold
- मीठा (Meetha) - sweet
- नमकीन (Namkeen) - salty
- तंग (Tang) - tight
- खुला (Khula) - open
- सुखा (Sukha) - dry
- तरबूज़ (Tarbooz) - watermelon
- अमेरिकी (American) - American
- भारतीय (Bhartiya) - Indian

Adverbs

Adverbs are an important part of speech in Hindi, used to modify verbs, adjectives, and other adverbs in a sentence. Here are some details about Hindi adverbs:

Modification: In Hindi, adverbs are used to modify the meaning of a verb, adjective, or another adverb in a sentence. For example, धीरे (dhire, slowly) modifies the verb चलना (chalna, walk) in the sentence वह धीरे चलता है (vah dhire chalta hai, he walks slowly).

Forms: In Hindi, adverbs do not change form based on gender, number, or case. However, some adverbs are formed by adding -ता (taa) to an adjective. For example, the adjective सुंदर (sundar, beautiful) becomes the adverb सुंदरता (sundarta, beautifully).

Types: Hindi adverbs can be classified into several categories based on their function in a sentence. These include adverbs of manner, adverbs of time, adverbs of frequency, adverbs of degree, and adverbs of place.

Usage: Adverbs of manner are used to describe how an action is performed, such as धीरे (dhire, slowly) or जल्दी (jaldi, quickly). Adverbs of time are used to indicate when an action takes place, such as अभी (abhi, now) or कल (kal, tomorrow). Adverbs of frequency are used to indicate how often an action takes place, such as हमेशा (hamesha, always) or कभी-कभी (kabhi-kabhi, sometimes). Adverbs of degree are used to modify adjectives or other adverbs, such as बहुत (bahut, very) or थोड़ा (thoda, a little). Adverbs of place are used to indicate where an action takes place, such as यहाँ (yahan, here) or वहाँ (vahan, there).

Comparison: In Hindi, some adverbs can be compared using the comparative and superlative forms. For example, the adverb धीरे (dhire, slowly) becomes धीरे-धीरे (dhire-dhire, more and more slowly) in the comparative form and सबसे धीरे (sabse dhire, the slowest) in the superlative form.

Formation: Some Hindi adverbs are formed by adding a suffix to a base word, such as जल्दी (jaldi, quickly) from जल्द (jald, quick) or सुबह (subah, in the morning) from सुबह (subaha, morning).

Usage with verbs: In Hindi, adverbs can be used to modify the meaning of a verb, such as indicating the manner in which an action is performed. For example, वह बड़ी से बड़ी लहर में समुद्र में तैरता है (vah badi se badi lahar mein samudr mein tairta hai, he swims in the ocean in big waves).

Usage with adjectives: In Hindi, adverbs can also be used to modify the meaning of an adjective, such as indicating the degree or intensity of the adjective. For example, वह बहुत ऊँचा है (vah bahut uncha hai, he is very tall).

Usage with other adverbs: In Hindi, adverbs can be used to modify the meaning of other adverbs. For example, वह बहुत धीरे चलता है (vah bahut dhire chalta hai, he walks very slowly).

Placement: In Hindi, adverbs usually come before the verb they modify. However, they can also be placed after the verb or at the beginning or end of the sentence for emphasis or to create a specific effect.

Negation: In Hindi, adverbs can be negated using the word नहीं (nahin, not). For example, वह जल्दी नहीं चलता है (vah jaldi nahin chalta hai, he does not walk quickly).

Inflection: Some Hindi adverbs can be inflected to indicate different degrees of intensity or comparison. For example, the adverb बहुत (bahut, very) can be inflected to बहुतीयत (bahutiyaat, extremely).

Here are some examples of adverbs in Hindi:

- शायद (Shayad) - perhaps
- भी (Bhi) - also
- कभी (Kabhi) - sometimes
- हमेशा (Hamesha) - always
- धीरे-धीरे (Dheere-dheere) - slowly
- तुरंत (Turant) - immediately
- धन्यवाद (Dhanyavaad) - thank you
- यहाँ (Yahaan) - here
- वहाँ (Vahaan) - there
- बहुत (Bahut) - very
- बिल्कुल (Bilkul) - absolutely
- बहुत जल्दी (Bahut jaldi) - very quickly
- वाकई (Vaakai) - really
- समय पर (Samay par) - on time
- देर से (Der se) - late
- सभी (Sabhi) - all
- बस (Bas) - just
- जरूर (Jaroor) - certainly
- आज कल (Aaj kal) - these days
- फिर (Phir) - again

Chapter 7: Verbs and Tenses

Verbs

Verbs are an important part of speech in Hindi, used to express an action or a state of being. Here are some details about Hindi verbs:

Agreement: In Hindi, verbs must agree with the subject of the sentence in gender, number, and person. For example, if the subject is masculine and singular, the verb must also be masculine and singular.

Tenses: Hindi verbs have three main tenses: present, past, and future. Each tense has two aspects: simple and continuous. The continuous aspect is formed by adding रहा/रही/रहे (raha/rahi/rahe) to the end of the verb stem.

Forms: In Hindi, verbs are usually conjugated by adding suffixes to the verb stem. The verb stem is usually formed by removing the infinitive ending -ना (-naa) from the base form of the verb.

Voice: Hindi verbs can be in either active or passive voice. In active voice, the subject performs the action, while in passive voice, the subject receives the action.

Mood: Hindi verbs can be in different moods, such as indicative, imperative, subjunctive, and conditional. The indicative mood is used to make statements or ask questions, while the imperative mood is used to give commands. The subjunctive mood is used to express doubt, uncertainty, or hypothetical situations. The conditional mood is used to express a condition or a possibility.

Auxiliaries: In Hindi, some verbs are used as auxiliary verbs to form the different tenses, such as होना (hona, to be) or जाना (jana, to go).

Usage: Hindi verbs can be used to express a wide range of actions and states of being, such as physical actions, mental processes, emotions, and changes in state.

Infinitives: In Hindi, the infinitive form of a verb ends in -ना (-naa). For example, the infinitive form of the verb खाना (khaana, to eat) is खाना (khaana).

Participles: In Hindi, there are two types of participles: present and past. The present participle is formed by adding -ता/-ती/-ते (-taa/ti/te) to the verb stem. The past participle is formed by adding -आ/-ई/-ए (-aa/ee/e) to the verb stem.

Gerunds: In Hindi, the gerund form of a verb ends in -कर (-kar). For example, the gerund form of the verb खाना (khaana, to eat) is खाकर (khaakar, by eating).

Compound Verbs: Hindi also has compound verbs, which are formed by combining two or more verbs to form a new word. For example, the compound verb देखकर बोलना (dekhkar bolna, to speak after seeing) combines the verbs देखना (dekhaana, to see) and बोलना (bolna, to speak) to form a new verb.

Idiomatic Expressions: Hindi verbs are also used in many idiomatic expressions, which can be difficult to translate directly into English. For example, the expression मुझे गुस्सा आता है (mujhe gussa aata hai, I get angry) literally translates to "anger comes to me."

Here are some examples of verbs in Hindi:

- जाना (Jana) - to go
- आना (Aana) - to come
- करना (Karna) - to do
- पढ़ना (Padhna) - to read
- लिखना (Likna) - to write
- खाना (Khana) - to eat
- पीना (Peena) - to drink
- बोलना (Bolna) - to speak
- देखना (Dekhna) - to see
- सुनना (Sunna) - to listen
- सोना (Sona) - to sleep
- उठना (Uthna) - to wake up
- बैठना (Baithna) - to sit
- खड़ा होना (Khada hona) - to stand
- जलाना (Jalana) - to burn
- बचाना (Bachana) - to save
- सीखना (Sikahna) - to learn
- खेलना (Khelna) - to play
- रोना (Rona) - to cry
- हंसना (Hansna) - to laugh

Tenses

Hindi has three primary tenses: present, past, and future. Each tense has two aspects: simple and continuous. Here are some details about each tense:

1. Present Tense: The present tense in Hindi is used to describe actions or states of being that are happening now or are habitual. It has two forms: simple present and present continuous.

    - Simple Present: The simple present tense is formed by adding the appropriate present tense marker to the end of the verb stem. For example, खाना (khaana, to eat) becomes खाता है (khaata hai, he eats).
    - Present Continuous: The present continuous tense is formed by adding रहा/रही/रहे (raha/rahi/rahe) to the present tense stem. For example, खा रहा है (kha raha hai, he is eating).

2. Past Tense: The past tense in Hindi is used to describe actions or states of being that have already happened. It has two forms: simple past and past continuous.

    - Simple Past: The simple past tense is formed by adding the appropriate past tense marker to the end of the verb stem. For example, खाना (khaana, to eat) becomes खाया (khaaya, he ate).
    - Past Continuous: The past continuous tense is formed by adding रहा/रही/रहे (raha/rahi/rahe) to the past tense stem. For example, खा रहा था (kha raha tha, he was eating).

3. Future Tense: The future tense in Hindi is used to describe actions or states of being that will happen in the future. It has two forms: simple future and future continuous.

- Simple Future: The simple future tense is formed by adding the appropriate future tense marker to the end of the verb stem. For example, खाना (khaana, to eat) becomes खाएगा (khaayega, he will eat).

- Future Continuous: The future continuous tense is formed by adding रहा/रही/रहे (raha/rahi/rahe) to the future tense stem. For example, खा रहा होगा (kha raha hoga, he will be eating).

4. Perfect Tenses: Hindi also has perfect tenses, which indicate completion of an action or state of being. The perfect tenses are formed using the auxiliary verb होना (hona, to be) in combination with the past participle of the main verb.

    - Present Perfect: The present perfect tense is formed by conjugating होना in the present tense and adding the past participle of the main verb. For example, खाना (khaana, to eat) becomes खा चुका है (kha chuka hai, he has eaten).
    - Past Perfect: The past perfect tense is formed by conjugating होना in the past tense and adding the past participle of the main verb. For example, खाना (khaana, to eat) becomes खा चुका था (kha chuka tha, he had eaten).
    - Future Perfect: The future perfect tense is formed by conjugating होना in the future tense and adding the past participle of the main verb. For example, खाना (khaana, to eat) becomes खा चुका होगा (kha chuka hoga, he will have eaten).

5. Conditional Tenses: Hindi also has conditional tenses, which are used to indicate hypothetical or uncertain situations. The conditional tenses are formed using the auxiliary verb होना in combination with the past participle of the main verb.

- Present Conditional: The present conditional tense is formed by conjugating होना in the present tense and adding the past participle of the main verb. For example, खाना (khaana, to eat) becomes खा सकता है (kha sakta hai, he could eat).
- Past Conditional: The past conditional tense is formed by conjugating होना in the past tense and adding the past participle of the main verb. For example, खाना (khaana, to eat) becomes खा सकता था (kha sakta tha, he could have eaten).

Chapter 8: Nouns and Articles

Nouns

A noun in Hindi is a word that refers to a person, place, thing, or idea.

Gender: In Hindi, all nouns are classified as masculine, feminine, or neuter. The gender of a noun determines the form of certain other words in the sentence, such as adjectives and verbs. For example, the noun लड़का (ladka, boy) is masculine, while the noun लड़की (ladki, girl) is feminine.

Number: Nouns in Hindi can be singular or plural. The plural form is usually formed by adding -एं (-en) to the singular form. For example, the singular form of लड़का (ladka, boy) becomes लड़के (ladke, boys) in the plural form.

Case: Nouns in Hindi can be in one of three cases: nominative, accusative, or oblique. The nominative case is used for the subject of a sentence, the accusative case is used for the direct object of a sentence, and the oblique case is used for all other uses, such as the indirect object, possessive, or vocative.

Declension: Hindi nouns are declined based on gender, number, and case. The declension pattern depends on the gender of the noun. There are four different declension patterns in Hindi: a-, i-, u-, and ī-stems.

Compound Nouns: Hindi also has compound nouns, which are formed by combining two or more nouns to form a new word. For example, अध्यापक (adhyapak, teacher) is a compound noun formed from अध्यापन (adhyapan, teaching) and पक्ष (paksh, side).

Possessive Forms: Possessive forms of Hindi nouns are formed by adding the appropriate possessive marker to the end of the noun. The possessive marker is usually -का (-ka) for masculine nouns, -की (-ki) for feminine nouns, and -के (-ke) for neuter nouns. For example, the possessive form of घर (ghar, house) is घर का (ghar ka, house's).

Common Nouns: Common nouns in Hindi refer to generic or non-specific people, places, things, or ideas. For example, आदमी (aadmi, man), स्थान (sthan, place), वस्तु (vastu, thing), विषय (vishay, topic).

Proper Nouns: Proper nouns in Hindi refer to specific people, places, things, or ideas. Proper nouns are always capitalized in Hindi. For example, राम (Ram), दिल्ली (Delhi), ताज महल (Taj Mahal).

Abstract Nouns: Abstract nouns in Hindi refer to concepts, feelings, or qualities that cannot be perceived through the senses. For example, प्रेम (prem, love), आत्मविश्वास (aatmavishwaas, self-confidence), शांति (shaanti, peace).

Collective Nouns: Collective nouns in Hindi refer to a group of individuals or things as a single entity. For example, सेना (sena, army), समूह (samuh, group), फलसेत (phalset, orchard).

Diminutive Nouns: Diminutive nouns in Hindi are formed by adding the suffix -ट्टा (-tta) to a noun to indicate a smaller or younger version of the noun. For example, घर (ghar, house) becomes घरट्टा (ghartta, small house).

Augmentative Nouns: Augmentative nouns in Hindi are formed by adding the suffix -ड़ा (-da) to a noun to indicate a larger or more impressive version of the noun. For example, घर (ghar, house) becomes घरड़ा (gharda, big house).

Usage: Nouns in Hindi are used extensively in communication, both in written and spoken forms. They are essential to forming complete sentences, and can be used to convey a wide range of meanings and contexts.

Here are some examples of nouns in Hindi:

- आदमी (Aadmi) - man
- स्त्री (Stri) - woman
- बच्चा (Baccha) - child
- घर (Ghar) - house
- आसमान (Aasmaan) - sky
- धूप (Dhoop) - sunlight
- वर्षा (Varsha) - rain
- सड़क (Sadak) - road
- पुस्तक (Pustak) - book
- दुकान (Dukaan) - shop
- फल (Phal) - fruit
- सब्जी (Sabzi) - vegetable
- दूध (Doodh) - milk
- रोटी (Roti) - bread
- चाय (Chai) - tea
- कॉफ़ी (Coffee) - coffee
- समाचार (Samaachaar) - news
- स्कूल (School) - school
- कॉलेज (College) - college
- विश्वविद्यालय (Vishvavidyalaya) – university

Articles

In Hindi grammar, articles are not used in the same way as they are in English. Hindi does not have separate words for "a" and "the," which are the two types of articles in English. Instead, Hindi uses the context of a sentence to determine whether a noun is definite or indefinite. Here's what you need to know about articles in Hindi:

Indefinite Articles: In Hindi, an indefinite noun is one that refers to any member of a class or group. For example, "a car" could be any car, not a specific one. To indicate an indefinite noun, Hindi speakers use the singular form of the noun, without any article. For example, "कुत्ता" (kutta) means "dog" or "a dog," depending on the context.

Definite Articles: In Hindi, a definite noun is one that refers to a specific person, place, or thing. To indicate a definite noun, Hindi speakers use the oblique case of the noun, which is formed by adding the suffix "को" (ko) to the end of the noun. For example, "घर" (ghar) means "house," while "घर को" (ghar ko) means "the house" or "that house."

Omission of Articles: In some cases, Hindi speakers may omit the article entirely. For example, in Hindi, there is no need to use the word "the" when talking about the sun or the moon, because these are considered to be universal entities. So, "the sun" would simply be "सूर्य" (soorya) and "the moon" would be "चांद" (chaand).

It's important to note that in Hindi, the context of a sentence is very important in determining whether a noun is definite or indefinite. For example, if you say "मैं घर जा रहा हूँ" (main ghar ja raha hoon), this means "I am going home." The noun "घर" (ghar, house) is indefinite in this context, because the speaker is not referring to a specific house. However, if you say "मैं उस घर में रहता हूँ" (main us ghar mein rehta hoon), this means "I live in that house." The noun "घर" (ghar, house) is definite in this context, because the speaker is referring to a specific house.

Here are some examples of articles in Hindi:

- एक (Ek) - a/an
- यह (Yah) - this
- वह (Vah) - that
- कुछ (Kuch) - some
- कोई (Koi) - any
- हर (Har) - every
- जो (Jo) - which
- कि (Ki) - that/which
- इस (Is) - this
- उस (Us) - that

Chapter 9: Questions and Negation

Questions

In Hindi language, questions can be formed in a few different ways. Here are some common types of questions in Hindi:

Interrogative Words: These are questions that use question words such as "kya" (what), "kaun" (who), "kab" (when), "kaise" (how), and "kyun" (why) to ask for information. For example, "तुम्हारी उम्र क्या है?" (tumhari umr kya hai?, what is your age?), "आप क्या काम करते हैं?" (aap kya kaam karte hain?, what do you do for a living?), or "आप कैसे हो?" (aap kaise ho?, how are you?).

Inverted Word Order: These are questions that have a verb-subject-object (VSO) or auxiliary-verb-subject-object (AVSO) word order, which is different from the typical subject-verb-object (SVO) word order in statements. For example, "क्या आप अंग्रेज़ी बोलते हैं?" (kya aap angrezi bolte hain?, do you speak English?), "क्या वे यहाँ आएँगे?" (kya ve yahaan aayenge?, will they come here?), or "क्या आपने कल परीक्षा दी थी?" (kya aapne kal pareeksha di thi?, did you take the exam yesterday?).

Tag Questions: These are questions that are added to the end of a statement to confirm or seek agreement. For example, "आप हिंदी बोलते हैं, ना?" (aap Hindi bolte hain, na?, you speak Hindi, right?), "उसका नाम राहुल है, ठीक है ना?" (uska naam Rahul hai, theek hai na?, his name is Rahul, isn't it?), or "तुम अच्छा खाना बनाते हो, न?" (tum achha khana banate ho, na?, you cook good food, don't you?).

Rising Tone: In Hindi, questions are often marked by a rising tone at the end of the sentence. This rising tone indicates that the sentence is a question, even if there are no question words or inverted word order. For example, "तुम्हारा नाम क्या है?" (tumhara naam kya hai?, what is your name?) and "तुम अच्छा खाना बनाते हो?" (tum achha khana banate ho?, do you cook good food?) both use rising intonation to indicate that they are questions.

Polite Forms: Hindi has formal and informal forms of address, and the choice of which to use can affect the form of questions. For example, if you are addressing someone formally, you might say "क्या आप कल से उपलब्ध होंगे?" (kya aap kal se uplabdh honge?, will you be available from tomorrow?) instead of "तुम कल से उपलब्ध होगे?" (tum kal se uplabdh hoge?, will you be available from tomorrow?). The use of the formal "आप" (aap) instead of the informal "तुम" (tum) changes the tone and politeness level of the question.

Embedded Questions: In some cases, Hindi questions can be embedded within a larger sentence or clause. For example, "मुझे नहीं पता कि तुम कहाँ जा रहे हो?" (mujhe nahin pata ki tum kahan ja rahe ho?, I don't know where you're going?) or "उसे यह पता नहीं कि वे कब लौटेंगे?" (use yah pata nahin ki ve kab lautenge?, he doesn't know when they'll return?). These questions are formed by using the same word order as a statement, but with rising intonation at the end of the question portion.

Here are some examples of questions in Hindi language:

- क्या आपका नाम क्या है? (kya aapka naam kya hai?) - What is your name?

- तुम्हारी उम्र क्या है? (tumhari umr kya hai?) - What is your age?

- आप कैसे हैं? (aap kaise hain?) - How are you?

- आप क्या काम करते हैं? (aap kya kaam karte hain?) - What do you do for a living?

- आप कहाँ से हो? (aap kahan se ho?) - Where are you from?

- क्या आप हिंदी बोलते हैं? (kya aap Hindi bolte hain?) - Do you speak Hindi?

- क्या आप अंग्रेज़ी बोलते हैं? (kya aap angrezi bolte hain?) - Do you speak English?

- क्या आप अपना मोबाइल नंबर बता सकते हैं? (kya aap apna mobile number bata sakte hain?) - Can you give me your mobile number?

- आपकी पसंदीदा खाने की चीज़ क्या है? (aapki pasandeeda khane ki cheez kya hai?) - What is your favorite food?

- आप क्या सोचते हैं? (aap kya sochte hain?) - What do you think?

Negation

Negation in Hindi language involves using negative words or particles to negate or deny a statement. Here are some key elements of negation in Hindi:

Negative Words: Hindi has several negative words that can be used to negate a statement. Some common examples include "नहीं" (nahin), "ना" (na), "मत" (mat), and "कोई नहीं" (koi nahin). These words can be used to negate verbs, nouns, and adjectives, depending on the context.

Particle "नहीं" (nahin): One of the most common ways to negate a statement in Hindi is to use the particle "नहीं" (nahin), which means "no" or "not". This particle is used after the verb or adjective that is being negated. For example, "मैं नहीं जाऊँगा" (main nahin jaaunga, I will not go), "वह कुछ नहीं खाती" (vah kuch nahin khaati, she does not eat anything), or "तुम्हारी उम्र कितनी है? - मेरी उम्र 25 नहीं है, 27 है" (tumhari umr kitni hai? - meri umr 25 nahin hai, 27 hai, what is your age? - my age is not 25, it's 27).

Particle "ना" (na): Another way to negate a statement in Hindi is to use the particle "ना" (na), which means "not" or "no". This particle is used after the noun or adjective that is being negated. For example, "यह फल अच्छा नहीं है" (yah phal achha nahin hai, this fruit is not good), "उसकी दुकान बंद नहीं हुई" (uski dukaan band nahin hui, his shop did not close), or "मैं खुश नहीं हूँ" (main khush nahin hoon, I am not happy).

Imperative "मत" (mat): The imperative form of the verb "करना" (karna, to do) is "करो" (karo, do), and the negative form of the imperative is "मत करो" (mat karo, don't do). This form is used to give a negative command or prohibition. For example, "मेरे पास से छुटकारा मत ढूँढो" (mere paas se chhootkara mat dhoondo, don't look for a way to get rid of me), "बहुत ज्यादा कुछ मत खाओ" (bahut jyaada kuch mat khao, don't eat too much), or "मत बात करो" (mat baat karo, don't talk).

Compound Negation: In Hindi, it is also possible to create a compound negation by using both a negative word and a negative particle together. For example, "कोई नहीं आया नहीं" (koi nahin aaya nahin, nobody came), "मैं कभी नहीं खाता नहीं" (main kabhi nahin khaata nahin, I never eat anything), or "तुम कुछ नहीं करते ना?" (tum kuch nahin karte na?, you don't do anything, right?).

Double Negation: In Hindi, it is common to use double negation to reinforce the negative meaning of a sentence. This is done by adding a negative word before the main negative particle, such as "कभी कोई नहीं आता" (kabhi koi nahin aata, nobody ever comes) or "उसके पास कुछ नहीं नहीं है" (uske paas kuch nahin nahin hai, he doesn't have anything at all).

Negative Questions: In Hindi, negative questions are formed by using the negative particle "नहीं" (nahin) or "ना" (na) at the end of a question. For example, "तुम कल नहीं आओगे?" (tum kal nahin aaoge?, won't you come tomorrow?) or "उसे कुछ पता ना है?" (use kuch pata na hai?, doesn't he know anything?). In negative questions, the rising tone at the end of the sentence is replaced by a falling tone.

Infinitive Forms: In Hindi, the infinitive forms of verbs are often used in negation. For example, "खाना नहीं बनाना" (khana nahin banana, not to cook food) or "जाना नहीं है" (jana nahin hai, not to go). This construction is useful for expressing negative commands or prohibitions.

Word Order: In Hindi, the position of negative particles and words can vary depending on the sentence structure. In simple statements, the negative particle is placed directly after the verb or adjective that is being negated. In more complex sentences, the negative particle may be placed before or after other parts of the sentence. For example, "मैं उसे कभी नहीं देखा हूँ" (main use kabhi nahin dekha hoon, I have never seen him) or "उसकी दुकान बंद नहीं हुई होगी" (uski dukaan band nahin hui hogi, his shop probably didn't close).

Here are some examples of negation in Hindi:

- मैं नहीं जाऊँगा। (Main nahin jaaunga.) - I will not go.

- वह कुछ नहीं खाती। (Vah kuch nahin khaati.) - She does not eat anything.

- यह फल अच्छा नहीं है। (Yah phal achha nahin hai.) - This fruit is not good.

- मेरी उम्र 25 नहीं है, 27 है। (Meri umr 25 nahin hai, 27 hai.) - My age is not 25, it's 27.

- तुम्हारे पास पैसे नहीं हैं। (Tumhare paas paise nahin hain.) - You don't have money.

- कोई नहीं आया नहीं। (Koi nahin aaya nahin.) - Nobody came.

- मैं कभी नहीं खाता नहीं। (Main kabhi nahin khaata nahin.) - I never eat anything.

- तुम कुछ नहीं करते ना? (Tum kuch nahin karte na?) - You don't do anything, right?

- उसकी दुकान बंद नहीं हुई। (Uski dukaan band nahin hui.) - His shop did not close.

- मत बात करो। (Mat baat karo.) - Don't talk.

Chapter 10: Idioms and Expressions

Idioms

Idioms in Hindi are commonly used expressions that are unique to the Hindi language. These expressions are made up of a group of words that are not meant to be taken literally. They often have a figurative meaning that cannot be understood by simply translating each word. Idioms are an important aspect of language and culture, as they reflect the values, beliefs, and customs of a community.

Here are some examples of idioms in Hindi along with their meanings:

- अपना अपना भाग्य होता है। (Apna apna bhagya hota hai.) - Everyone has their own destiny.

- जितनी चादर हो उतने ही पैर फैलाने चाहिए। (Jitni chadar ho, utne hi pair phailane chahiye.) - Stretch your legs only as much as the blanket allows. (Spend within your means.)

- जैसे को तैसा। (Jaise ko taisa.) - As you sow, so shall you reap.

- हरियाली अमेरिका जाने से कम नहीं है। (Hariyaali America jaane se kam nahin hai.) - There's no place like home.

- आपा खोये, गिरी लाठी संभाल नहीं पाए। (Aapa khoye, giri laathi sambhaal nahin paaye.) - When you lose your own, you can't handle a fallen stick. (Unable to take care of oneself when in trouble.)

- अंगूठा छोड़ना (Angootha chhodna) - To back out or retreat from a situation. (Literally, to let go of one's thumb)
- अंधों में काना राजा (Andhon mein kaana raja) - In the land of the blind, the one-eyed man is king. (Literal meaning: In a group of blind people, the person with one eye can be the ruler.)
- अपना उल्लू सीधा करना (Apna ullu seedha karna) - To act smart or make oneself look wise. (Literal meaning: To straighten one's own owl)
- अपने पराये का दमन नहीं करना (Apne paraye ka daman nahin karna) - To not interfere in someone else's affairs. (Literal meaning: To not hold onto someone else's clothes)
- बंदर क्या जाने अदरक का स्वाद (Bandar kya jaane adark ka swaad) - A monkey doesn't know the taste of ginger. (Literal meaning: The monkey doesn't know how ginger tastes.)
- अँधे की लाठी, बहरे का बजना। (Andhe ki laathi, behre ka bajna) - This means that sometimes, people who are not qualified for a job or task get it, while others who are more qualified miss out.
- जल में रहकर मगर से बैर ठीक नहीं। (Jal mein rehkar magar se bair theek nahin) - This means that you should not hold a grudge against someone if you are dependent on them.
- कहा तलवार की छाल में निहार? (Kaha talwar ki chaal mein nihaar?) - This means that you should look at things carefully before making a decision.

Expressions

Expressions in Hindi refer to any words or phrases that convey a particular meaning or sentiment. These expressions may include idioms, phrases, proverbs, similes, and metaphors, among others. Expressions are an important aspect of any language, as they help to convey complex ideas and emotions in a concise and meaningful way. Expressions in Hindi are often used in daily conversations and can add depth and nuance to communication.

Here are some examples of expressions in Hindi along with their meanings:

- जल जाना (Jal jana) - To feel jealous or envious. (Literal meaning: To get burnt or scalded)

- हाथ का मेल होना (Haath ka mel hona) - To have a good rapport or understanding with someone. (Literal meaning: To have the same texture in your hands)

- बोझ उठाना (Bojh uthana) - To take responsibility for something. (Literal meaning: To lift a burden)

- बैंगन का भरता (Baingan ka bharta) - To do something without any significant outcome or result. (Literal meaning: Mashed eggplant)

- उलटा चोर कोतवाल को संगत (Ulat chor kotwal ko sangat) - If a criminal is appointed as a police officer, he can be of great help to other criminals. (Literal meaning: An inverted thief can be a good companion to the policeman.)

- खट्टी मीठी यादें (Khatti meethi yaadein) - Memories that are both sweet and sour.

- कान काटना (Kaam kaato) - To eavesdrop on someone's conversation. (Literal meaning: To cut someone's work)

- कलम हटाना (Kalam hataana) - To change one's mind. (Literal meaning: To remove the pen)

- चार दिन की चांदनी फिर अंधेरी रात (Chaardhin ki chaandni phir andheri raat) - To describe a brief period of happiness followed by a long period of sadness. (Literal meaning: Four days of moonlight, then a dark night.)

- कौवा चला हंस की चाल (Kauva chala hans ki chaal) - To copy someone's way of doing things without understanding the true meaning behind it. (Literal meaning: The crow walks like a swan)

Chapter 11: Writing System

The writing system of the Hindi language is based on the Devanagari script, which is an abugida (alphasyllabary) writing system. Devanagari is derived from the Brahmi script, which is one of the oldest known writing systems in the world.

The Devanagari script consists of 47 primary characters, which include 14 vowels and 33 consonants. The vowels are written as independent characters or as diacritics above or below the consonants, while the consonants are written as standalone characters. In addition, there are several conjunct consonants, which are formed by combining two or more consonants.

The Devanagari script is written from left to right and is used to write several languages, including Hindi, Marathi, Nepali, and Sanskrit. The script is highly phonetic, meaning that the characters correspond to specific sounds in the language. This makes it easier for learners to read and write Hindi, as there is a direct correspondence between the spoken and written forms of the language.

In addition to the primary characters, the Devanagari script also includes various punctuation marks, such as the full stop (पूर्ण विराम - poorn viram), comma (अर्ध विराम - ardha viram), and question mark (प्रश्न चिह्न - prashn chinh).

In the Devanagari script, the consonants are organized according to the place and manner of articulation. The place of articulation refers to where in the mouth the sound is produced, while the manner of articulation refers to how the sound is produced.

The consonants are organized into five groups, based on the place of articulation:

- Velar consonants: These are pronounced using the back of the tongue and the soft palate. Examples include क (ka), ख (kha), ग (ga), and घ (gha).
- Palatal consonants: These are pronounced using the front of the tongue and the hard palate. Examples include च (cha), छ (chha), ज (ja), and झ (jha).
- Retroflex consonants: These are pronounced using the tip of the tongue curled back towards the roof of the mouth. Examples include ट (Ta), ठ (Tha), ड (Da), and ढ (Dha).
- Dental consonants: These are pronounced using the teeth and the tongue. Examples include त (ta), थ (tha), द (da), and ध (dha).
- Labial consonants: These are pronounced using the lips. Examples include प (pa), फ (pha), ब (ba), and भ (bha).

In addition to the consonants, the Devanagari script also includes various vowel marks (matras) that are used to modify the sound of the consonants. There are three types of matras: short vowels (a, i, u), long vowels (aa, ii, uu), and diphthongs (ai, au).

One of the unique features of the Devanagari script is the way it represents the sound of the nasal consonants. In Hindi, there are three nasal consonants - न (n), म (m), and ङ (ng). When a nasal consonant is followed by a plosive consonant (such as क, ट, च), the sound of the nasal consonant is represented by a dot called the Anusvara (ं) above the consonant. For example, the word "कंप्यूटर" (computer) is written as क-ं-प्-यू-ट-र in Devanagari script.

Similarly, when a nasal consonant is followed by a fricative consonant (such as फ, थ, श), the sound of the nasal consonant is represented by a curly line called the Chandrabindu (ँ) above the consonant. For example, the word "अँग्रेज़ी" (English) is written as अ-ँ-ग्-रे-ज़-ी in Devanagari script.

Learning the Devanagari script is an important step in becoming proficient in reading and writing Hindi, as it allows learners to accurately represent the sounds of the language. It may take some practice to become comfortable with the script, but with time and dedication, learners can develop the skills necessary to use it effectively.

Chapter 12: Honorfics in Hindi

Honorifics in Hindi are words or expressions that are used to show respect and politeness to someone. In Hindi, honorifics are an important aspect of communication, particularly when addressing people who are older, in positions of authority, or who are considered to be higher in social status.

Some of the most common honorifics used in Hindi include:

- जी (ji) - This is a suffix that is added to the end of a person's name or title to show respect. For example, "Namaste ji" (नमस्ते जी) is a common greeting used to show respect to someone.

- आप (aap) - This is a formal way of addressing someone and is used to show respect. It is commonly used when addressing elders or people in positions of authority.

- श्री (shree) - This is a prefix that is added to the beginning of a person's name to show respect. It is commonly used when addressing someone in a formal or professional setting.

- संत (sant) - This is a title used to address religious leaders, particularly those who are considered to be saints or gurus.

- जनाब (janaab) - This is a title used to address someone in a formal or respectful manner. It is commonly used in Urdu and is also used in Hindi.

In addition to the honorifics mentioned above, there are also a number of other ways that Hindi speakers show respect to others. For example, when addressing someone who is older or in a position of authority, it is common to use the plural form of "you" (आप - aap) instead of the singular form (तुम - tum). This is seen as a sign of respect and deference.

Another way that Hindi speakers show respect is by using polite forms of verbs when speaking to others. For example, the verb "to go" in Hindi is जाना (jaana). When speaking to someone in a polite or formal context, the verb is conjugated as जाइए (jaiye) instead of जाओ (jao), which is the informal form.

Similarly, when asking a question in a formal or polite context, it is common to use the word क्या (kya) at the beginning of the sentence to show respect. For example, instead of saying "तुम कैसे हो?" (tum kaise ho?) which is informal, one would say "क्या आप कैसे हैं?" (kya aap kaise hain?) which is the polite form.

Understanding the appropriate use of honorifics and other forms of respect is an important part of learning Hindi, particularly if you plan to communicate with native speakers in a formal or professional context. By using the appropriate language and expressions, you can show respect and build positive relationships with others.

Chapter 13: Slang and Colloquialisms

Slang and Colloquialisms are informal words or phrases that are commonly used in everyday conversation. These words and phrases can add color and flavor to a conversation and are often used to convey a particular emotion or attitude.

Some common examples include:

- बकवास (bakwaas) - This is a slang word that means "nonsense" or "rubbish". It is commonly used to dismiss something that someone has said as being unimportant or untrue.

- फट्टू (fattu) - This is a slang word that is used to describe someone who is timid or cowardly. It is often used as an insult, particularly among young people.

- छोटू (chhotu) - This is a slang word that is used to refer to someone who is short or small in stature. It can be used as a playful nickname or as an insult, depending on the context.

- चुटकुला (chutkula) - This is a slang word that means "joke" or "pun". It is often used to tell a funny story or to add humor to a conversation.

- चंगा (changa) - This is a slang word that means "good" or "fine". It is commonly used in Punjabi and Hindi slang.

- बच्चा (bachcha) - This is a slang word that is used to refer to someone who is younger or less experienced.

- बात बन जाना (baat ban jaana) - This phrase is commonly used to refer to a situation where two people agree on something or come to a mutual understanding. It can be translated to mean "to come to an understanding".

- चलो न (chalo na) - This phrase is commonly used to express reluctance or unwillingness to do something. It can be translated to mean "let's not".

- कुछ भी (kuch bhi) - This phrase is commonly used to express disbelief or to indicate that something is absurd or ridiculous. It can be translated to mean "anything".

- जमानत लगाना (jamanat lagaana) - This phrase is commonly used to refer to the act of securing bail. It can be translated to mean "to apply for bail".

It is important to note that while slang and colloquialisms can add color and humor to a conversation, they may not be appropriate in all contexts. It is important to use discretion when using these words and to be mindful of the people around you.

Chapter 14: Hindi Vocabulary

Animals vocabulary

- बिल्ली (billi) - Cat
- कुत्ता (kutta) - Dog
- भेड़ (bhed) - Sheep
- गाय (gai) - Cow
- हिरण (hiran) - Deer
- घोड़ा (ghoda) - Horse
- शेर (sher) - Lion
- बाघ (bagh) - Tiger
- मछली (machhli) - Fish
- मदार (madar) - Monkey
- हाथी (haathi) - Elephant
- भालू (bhalu) - Bear
- खरगोश (khargosh) - Rabbit
- मोर (mor) – Peacock
- कछुआ (kachhua) - Turtle
- चींटी (cheenti) - Ant
- छिपकली (chipkali) - Lizard
- मगरमच्छ (magarmachh) - Crocodile
- मकड़ी (makdi) - Spider
- पिल्ला (pilla) - Puppy
- साँप (saap) - Snake
- सिंह (singh) – Lion

Family vocabulary

- परिवार (parivaar) - Family
- माता (maata) - Mother
- पिता (pita) - Father
- बेटी (beti) - Daughter
- बेटा (beta) - Son
- दादा (daada) - Paternal grandfather
- दादी (daadi) - Paternal grandmother
- नाना (naana) - Maternal grandfather
- नानी (naani) - Maternal grandmother
- भाई (bhai) - Brother
- बहन (behen) - Sister
- छोटा भाई (chhota bhai) - Younger brother
- छोटी बहन (chhoti behen) - Younger sister
- बड़ा भाई (bada bhai) - Older brother
- बड़ी बहन (badi behen) - Older sister
- ससुर (sasur) - Father-in-law
- सास (saas) - Mother-in-law
- जेठ (jeth) - Elder brother-in-law
- देवर (devar) - Younger brother-in-law
- भाभी (bhabhi) - Brother's wife or wife's brother's wife
- ननद (nanad) - Husband's sister
- साला (saala) - Wife's brother
- साली (saali) - Brother's wife or wife's brother's wife
- पत्नी (patni) - Wife
- पति (pati) – Husband

Time vocabulary

- समय (samay) - Time
- वर्ष (varsh) - Year
- महीना (mahina) - Month
- हफ्ता (hafta) - Week
- दिन (din) - Day
- घंटा (ghanta) - Hour
- मिनट (minute) - Minute
- सेकंड (second) - Second
- अर्धरात्रि (ardhraatri) - Midnight
- सुबह (subah) - Morning
- दोपहर (dopahar) - Afternoon
- शाम (shaam) - Evening
- रात (raat) - Night
- बजे (baje) - O'clock
- कल (kal) - Tomorrow
- आज (aaj) - Today
- पहले (pehle) - Before
- बाद में (baad mein) - Later
- अभी (abhi) - Now
- तुरंत (turant) - Immediately
- बस अभी (bas abhi) - Just now
- सबसे पहले (sabse pehle) - First of all
- दोबारा (dobara) - Again
- रोज़ (roz) - Daily
- हमेशा (hamesha) - Always
- कभी-कभी (kabhi-kabhi) - Sometimes
- अक्सर (aksar) – Often

Colors vocabulary

- लाल (laal) - Red
- नीला (neela) - Blue
- हरा (hara) - Green
- पीला (peela) - Yellow
- काला (kaala) - Black
- सफेद (safed) - White
- भूरा (bhura) - Brown
- गुलाबी (gulaabi) – Pink
- सोना (sona) - Gold
- चांदी (chaandi) - Silver
- ब्रॉन्ज (bronze) – Bronze

Shapes vocabulary

- वर्तुल (vartul) - Circle
- वृत्त (vritt) - Circle
- वर्ग (varg) - Square
- आयत (aayat) - Rectangle
- त्रिभुज (tribhuj) - Triangle
- समचतुर्भुज (samachaturbhuj) - Quadrilateral
- त्रिकोण (trikon) - Triangle
- अंडाकार (andaakaar) - Oval
- लंबवृत्त (lambavritt) - Ellipse
- स्तंभ (stambh) - Column
- गोला (gola) - Sphere
- बेलन (belan) – Cylinder

Weather vocabulary

- मौसम (mausam) - Weather
- बारिश (baarish) - Rain
- बर्फ (barf) - Snow
- धूप (dhoop) - Sun
- आँधी (aandhi) - Storm
- तूफ़ान (toofan) - Hurricane
- सूखा (sookha) - Drought
- बदल (badal) - Cloud
- बारिश का पानी (baarish ka paani) - Rainwater
- तापमान (taapmaan) - Temperature
- मौसमी बदलाव (mausami badlaav) - Weather changes
- मौसम की ताज़गी (mausam ki taazgi) - Freshness of the weather
- ठंड (thand) - Cold
- गर्मी (garmi) - Heat
- सर्दी (sardi) - Winter
- गर्मी का मौसम (garmi ka mausam) - Summer
- मृदु (mridu) - Soft
- बहुत गर्म (bahut garm) - Very hot

Transportation vocabulary

- ट्रेन (train) - Train
- बस (bus) - Bus
- मोटरसाइकिल (motorcycle) - Motorcycle
- स्कूटर (scooter) - Scooter
- कार (car) - Car
- जहाज़ (jahaz) - Ship
- हवाई जहाज़ (hawai jahaz) - Airplane
- हेलीकॉप्टर (helicopter) - Helicopter
- साइकिल (cycle) - Bicycle
- ट्रक (truck) - Truck
- ट्रैक्टर (tractor) - Tractor
- टेक्सी (taxi) - Taxi
- रिक्शा (riksha) - Rickshaw
- बाइक (bike) - Bike

Food vocabulary

- भोजन (bhojan) - Food
- दाल (daal) - Lentils
- चावल (chaawal) - Rice
- रोटी (roti) - Bread
- सब्ज़ी (sabzi) - Vegetables
- मछली (machli) - Fish
- चिकन (chicken) - Chicken
- मटन (mutton) - Lamb
- पनीर (paneer) - Cottage cheese
- दही (dahi) - Yogurt
- गुड़ (gud) - Jaggery
- जीरा (jeera) - Cumin
- हल्दी (haldi) - Turmeric
- मिठाई (mithai) - Sweet
- दूध (doodh) - Milk
- मक्खन (makhan) - Butter
- रस्सा (rassa) - Gravy
- चाय (chai) - Tea
- कॉफ़ी (coffee) - Coffee
- खजूर (khajur) - Dates
- खीर (kheer) - Rice pudding

Fruits vocabulary

- फल (phal) - Fruit
- आम (aam) - Mango
- सेब (seb) - Apple
- केला (kela) - Banana
- संतरा (santara) - Orange
- अंगूर (angoor) - Grapes
- अनार (anaar) - Pomegranate
- अमरूद (amrood) - Guava
- जामुन (jamun) - Indian blackberry
- लीची (lihchi) - Lychee
- पपीता (papita) - Papaya
- नाशपाती (nashpati) - Pear
- तरबूज (tarbuj) - Watermelon
- खरबूजा (kharbuja) - Muskmelon
- कीवी (kiwi) - Kiwi
- नींबू (nimbu) - Lemon
- अंजीर (anjeer) - Fig
- खुबानी (khubani) - Apricot
- सीताफल (sitafal) - Custard apple
- टामेटो (tameto) - Tomato
- केलीफ़्लावर (keliflavar) - Pineapple

Vegetables vocabulary

- सब्ज़ी (sabzi) - Vegetables
- आलू (aaloo) - Potato
- गाजर (gaajar) - Carrot
- गोभी (gobhi) - Cauliflower
- मटर (matar) - Peas
- फूलगोभी (phoolgobhi) - Broccoli
- टमाटर (tamatar) - Tomato
- बैंगन (baingan) - Eggplant
- प्याज़ (pyaaz) - Onion
- शलगम (shalgam) - Turnip
- लौकी (lauki) - Bottle gourd
- कद्दू (kaddu) - Pumpkin
- पालक (paalak) - Spinach
- मेथी (methi) - Fenugreek
- भिंडी (bhindi) - Okra
- ककड़ी (kakdi) - Cucumber
- हरी मिर्च (hari mirch) - Green chili

Emotions vocabulary

- खुशी (khushi) - Happiness
- दुख (dukh) - Sadness
- गुस्सा (gussa) - Anger
- शर्म (sharm) - Embarrassment/Shame
- डर (dar) - Fear
- आशा (aasha) - Hope
- शांति (shaanti) - Peace
- उत्साह (utsaah) - Enthusiasm
- उम्मीद (umeed) - Expectation/Hope
- निराशा (niraasha) - Disappointment
- खिलखिलाहट (khilkhilaahat) - Joy/Laughter
- रोमांच (romaanch) - Thrill/Excitement
- संतोष (santosh) - Satisfaction
- चिंता (chinta) - Worry
- आक्रोश (aakrosh) - Rage/Outrage
- ख़तरनाकी (khatarnaakii) - Danger
- ग़म (gham) - Grief/Sorrow
- उदासी (udaasi) - Melancholy
- निराशा (niraashaa) - Hopelessness
- शोक (shok) - Mourning

www.ingramcontent.com/pod-product-compliance
Lightning Source LLC
Chambersburg PA
CBHW032017290426
44109CB00013B/694